Introduction

An essential ingredient for any family get-together, or party, is a good selection of games to play. With a little thought and planning, games can help to provide amusement for all concerned, and provide a welcome break during the proceedings.

The Scotsman Children's Party Games is a fascinating, highly illustrated guide to almost 150 games and activities, most of which can be played by children over the age of five, and by adults of any age. Each game details the minimum age group, the optimum number of players, the aim of the game, any preparation required, and the various stages in the game itself. With each activity there are step-by-step instructions and clear, accurate diagrams showing techniques and methods that are easy to follow.

The games are arranged under specific categories, such as action, musical, racing, dice or spoken word games, and include old favourites such as Hide and Seek and Pin the Tail on the Donkey, as well as newer activities. Additionally, to make finding the right game easy, this book includes indexes of games by appropriate age and games defined by a certain number of players.

Contents

Games by Age

Games for age 3+

Games for age 5+

Games for age 5–10

Games for age 7+

Games for age 8+

Games for age 9+

Games for age 10+

Games by Players

Games for 2 players

Games for groups of players

Games for teams of players

Action Games

MY LITTLE BIRD

Age 3+ **Players Group**

This game is played in countries all over the world. Other names for it include Flying High and Birds Fly.

Play

- One player is the leader and the others stand in a row in front of him. Alternatively, everyone sits around a table.
- The leader starts by saying 'My little bird is lively, is lively,' and then goes on to name something followed by the word 'fly' – for example, he might say 'eggs fly.' 
- If whatever he names can fly – for example, cockatoos – the players raise their arms and wave them about. If it cannot fly – as with eggs – the players should remain still.
- A player who makes a mistake is out. The last player left in the game wins.

CHARADES

Age 7+

Players Teams

Charades is probably the best-known and most popular of all games involving acting.

AIM

For one team to guess a word with several syllables, or the title of a book or film, that are acted out in mime by another team.

EQUIPMENT

Some dressing-up clothes will add to the fun but are not absolutely necessary.

PREPARATION

It is probably a good idea to prepare some good subjects beforehand if children are involved. Good examples include words such as Bandage, Carpet, Earring and Knapsack, or film and book titles.

PLAY

- The first team chooses its title or word and indicates the type of subject using one of the set mimes shown here. The team then indicates how many words and syllables the title contains by holding up fingers. It then acts out each word or syllable separately, or the whole word or title together. There are several ways of giving clues, such as indicating a short word, the word 'the', or the word of the title sounds like the one being mimed.

- The second team tries to guess what the word or title is.
- The game is played in turn by the teams, with the team with most correct guesses the winner.

Television

Play/theatre

Film

Book **Song/musical**

Sounds like

Number of words

Number of syllables

Small word

'The'

HIDE AND SEEK

Age 7+ **Players Group**

One of the best-loved and most enduring of all children's games.

Aim

To get 'home' without being touched.

Play

- One player is made 'seeker' and covers his or her eyes and counts to 40 while the others go and hide.
- The seeker then has to try to find players and touch them.
- The players must try to reach home without being touched – better still, without being seen by the seeker. The players who are caught are out.
- The last player to be caught is the winner and can take the place of the seeker.

HUNT THE THIMBLE

Age 5+ **Players Group**

This very popular game is usually played with a thimble, but any other small object will do.

Play

- All the players but one leave the room while the player left behind hides the thimble somewhere in the room or on his or her person. He then calls the other players back into the room to look for it.

- The game is won by the first player to find the thimble and take it to the player who hid it. The finder then has a turn at hiding the thimble.

IN THE MANNER OF THE WORD

Age 9+ **Players Group**

This is an amusing acting game in which players attempt to guess adverbs.

PLAY

- One player chooses an adverb, such as rapidly, quietly or amusingly. The other players in turn then ask him to carry out some action 'in the manner of the word'. For example, a player might say; 'Eat in the manner of the word,' 'Walk in the manner of the word,' or 'Laugh in the manner of the word.'
- The player who chooses the adverb must do as the other players ask, and the other players may make guesses as soon as acting begins.
- The first player to guess an adverb correctly scores one point. If no one guesses the word after each of the players has asked for an action, the player who chose the adverb receives one point.
- The game is won by the player with most points after each of the players has had a turn at choosing the adverb.

MATCHING PAIRS

Age 5–10

Players Group

EQUIPMENT

A number of everyday articles are needed and some wrapping paper.

PREPARATION

The host thinks of a 'pair' of items for each of the guests. Examples might include: salt and pepper, knife and fork, sock and shoe, a pair of gloves, a cup and saucer, a King and Queen (from a set of playing cards). The host wraps up one part of each 'pair' and hides the other somewhere in the room.

PLAY

- Players are given a part of their 'pair'.
- They have to look for what they think is likely to be the other, which has been hidden by the host.
- Every player who matches his pair within ten minutes or so is a winner.

SARDINES

Age 7+ **Players Group**

This is a type of Hide and Seek usually played in the dark. The more rooms that can be played in the more exciting the game becomes.

AIM

To find and join the 'sardine'.

PLAY

- One player is chosen as 'sardine' to go and hide (preferably somewhere big enough for most of the others to squeeze in, too) while all the others cover their eyes and count to 30.
- The seekers then go off individually to find the sardine.
- When a seeker locates the sardine, he or she joins the sardine in the hiding place. Eventually the hiding place is full of hiders, while fewer and fewer seekers remain.
- There are no winners in this game. The last player to find the hiding place is the next sardine.

SIMON SAYS

Age 3+

Players
Group

This is an old game and still a favourite.

PLAY

- One player is the leader and the others spread around in front of him or her.
- The leader orders the others to make various actions – such as touching their toes or raising their arms. Whether or not they must obey depends on how the orders are given.
- If the leader begins the order with the words 'Simon says,' the players must obey.. If he does not, they must not make the action. If a player makes a mistake, they are out of the game. The leader can encourage mistakes by giving rapid orders or by developing a rhythm and then breaking it.
- The last person left in the game is the winner and becomes the next leader.

TRIANGULAR TUG-OF-WAR

Age 10+ **Players Group**

Equipment

A 2–3 m (6–9 ft) length of rope (or cord) and three handkerchiefs are required.

Preparation

Tie the ends of the rope together. Make sure you have a large area clear of furniture. Get three players to stand outside the rope and hold it with one hand behind them to form a triangle. Place a handkerchief in front of each player.

Play

- The players have to hold on to the rope behind them and pick up the handkerchief in front of them. Each should be aware of his opponents though, and pull the rope to make sure they don't get to their handkerchiefs first.
- The player who manages to pick up his handkerchief first, while holding on to the rope, wins.

Ball Games

BUCKET BALL

Age 3+ **Players Group**

Aim

To get the ball into the bucket.

Play

- A plastic household bucket is weighed down with a large stone or brick.
- Players stand around it and take turns to throw a ball into it. Young players can stand fairly close, older ones further back. For players who are good at it, a smaller ball can be used since this makes the game more of a challenge.
- The player who gets the ball into the bucket most often wins.

FRENCH CRICKET

Age 10+ **Players Group**

EQUIPMENT

A tennis ball and tennis racket or cricket bat are needed.

PLAY

- Each player takes a turn at holding the racket or bat.
- Another player then tries to get him or her out by bowling and hitting his or her legs below the knees. The batter, meanwhile, protects the legs with the bat or racket and tries to hit the ball. Each time a player hits the ball, he or she scores a point and has another turn.
- If the batter hits the ball, he or she can face the way the ball will be coming from next. If not, he or she has to stay in the same position, making it difficult to protect the legs if the ball is coming from behind.
- The ball must be bowled from where it lands.
- A player who is hit below the knees is out.

GUARD THE GATE

Age 5–10 Players Group

AIM
To roll a ball through the 'gate' formed by the space between players.

PLAY
- Players form a circle, each being one arm's length away from the next. The gate is the space to his or her right.
- The ball (a tennis ball would be suitable, or a larger ball for younger players) is rolled by hand by the players, each trying to send it through any of the spaces between players – the gates. At the same time the players must guard their own gates to stop the ball going through. Players who let the ball through their gates drop out.
- The player who succeeds in defending his or her gate the longest wins.

HOT POTATO

Age 5–10 **Players Group**

Aim

For the players to keep the ball away from the player in the middle.

Play

- The players form a circle and one is chosen to stand in the centre.
- The ball is thrown from player to player, and the one in the middle tries to intercept. He or she may win the ball by touching it at any time, even if one of the other players is holding it, or it falls outside the circle. Whoever makes the mistake that allows the player in the middle to touch the ball takes his or her place.

- The game goes on until all the players have a turn in the middle. The one who holds out longest may be declared the winner.

Blindfold Games

BLIND MAN'S BLUFF

Age 7+ **Players Group**

Aim

A blindfolded player tries to catch and identify another player.

Play

- A blind person is chosen and blindfolded. He or she is turned around three times in the centre of the room and then left alone.
- The other players dance around, taunting the blindfolded person and dodging out of his or her way to avoid capture.
- When the blindfolded person catches someone, he or she has two or three guesses at the name of the prisoner. If correct, the prisoner becomes the new blind man. If wrong, he continues as the blind man and tries to catch another player.

BLIND MAN'S TREASURE HUNT

Age 7+ **Players Group**

Equipment

Parcels of different sizes and shapes, at least one for each player, plus several extra to allow choice for all players, and a blindfold, are needed.

Preparation
All the players must be sent out of the room. The parcels are then placed on a table in the middle of the room.

Play
- Bring in the guests one by one, blindfolded.
- Lead them up to the table and tell them they may choose one present, but must not open it until everyone has chosen.
- Everyone 'wins' something in this game. The fun lies in the opening of the presents, and guessing what they are from their shape and sound.

PIN THE TAIL ON THE DONKEY

Age 5+ **Players Group**

Aim
Blindfolded players try to pin a tail in the correct position on a drawing of a tail-less donkey.

Preparation
The organiser draws a large picture of a donkey without a tail and fastens it onto a pinboard propped upright. He also makes a donkey's tail out of cardboard or wool and sticks a large pin through the body end.

Play
- Each player in turn is blindfolded and turned around so that he is in front of and facing the donkey. He is then given the tail and attempts to

pin it on the correct part of the donkey.

- The organiser marks the position of each player's attempt.
- The player who pins nearest the correct place is the winner.

SQUEAK-PIGGY-SQUEAK

Age 7+ **Players Group**

AIM

A blindfolded player attempts to identify another player by getting him to squeak.

PLAY

- One player is blindfolded, given a cushion, and turned around three times in the centre of the room. The others sit down around the room.
- The blindfolded person must then place his or her cushion on another player's lap and sit on it, and then call 'squeak-piggy-squeak'. The person he or she is sitting on squeaks like a pig.
- If the blindfolded person recognises the person, they change places. Once the new person is blindfolded, the players all change seats before he or she tries to sit on a player's lap.

Contest Games

APPLE BOBBING

Age 5+ **Players Group**

EQUIPMENT

A large bowl, lots of apples, newspapers (in case of spillage) and a towel are needed.

PREPARATION

Fill the bowl with water, place it on newspapers and put a number of apples into the water.

PLAY

- Players take turns in trying to retrieve an apple from the bowl, using only their mouths.
- There are no real winners, since everybody should end up with an apple. Perhaps a small prize could be given to the player who gets his or her apple in the shortest time.

BATTLESHIPS

Age 10+ **Players 2**

AIM

The objective is to destroy an opponent's entire fleet by a series of 'hits'.

PLAY

- The players should sit so that they cannot see each other's papers. Each of them draws two identical playing areas, 10 squares by 10 squares in size. To identify each square, the playing areas have numbers down one side and letters across the top (thus the top left-hand square is A1; the bottom left-hand square is A10, etc.).
- Each player marks one playing area his or her 'home fleet' and the other playing area the 'enemy fleet'. Players have their own fleet of ships that they may position anywhere within their home fleet area. A fleet comprises:

  a) one battleship, four squares long;

  b) two cruisers, each three squares long;

  c) three destroyers, each two squares long; and

  d) four submarines, each one square only.

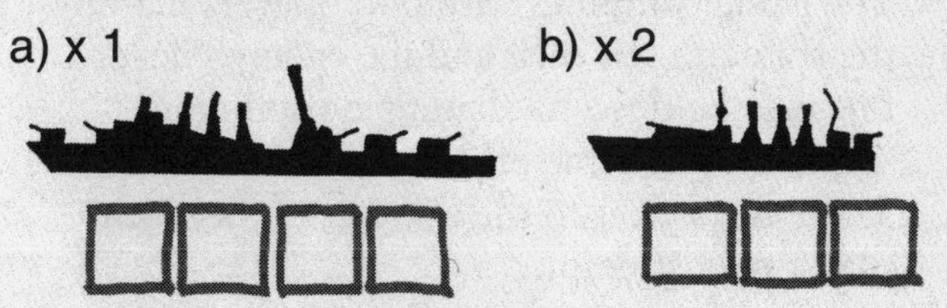

- Players 'position' their ships by outlining the appropriate number of squares. The squares representing each ship must be in a row or column (see page 66). There must also be at least one vacant square between ships. Players take turns.

- In each turn, a player may attempt three hits: he or she calls out the names of any three squares, marking them on the enemy fleet area as he or she does so.

- The player's opponent must then consult his or her own home fleet area to see whether any of these squares are occupied.

- If they are, he or she must state how many and the category of ship hit. In order to sink a ship, every one of its component squares must receive a hit.

- The game continues with both players marking the state of their own and the enemy's fleet – this may be done by shading or outlining squares, or in some other manner (see opposite). There is no limit to the number of hits each player may attempt.

- The winner is the player who first destroys his or her opponent's fleet.

Battleships: Player 1's positions

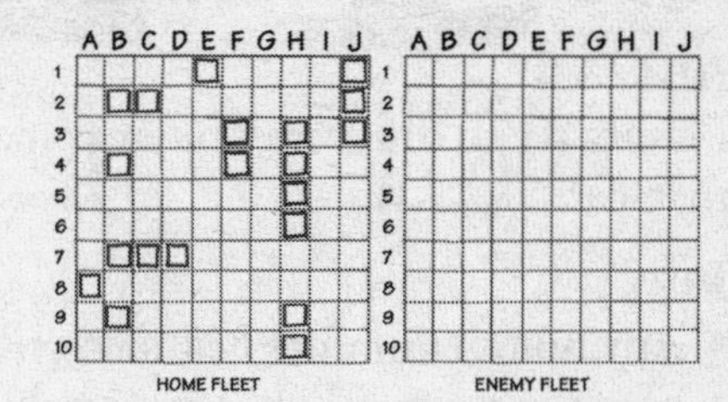

Battleships: Player 2's positions

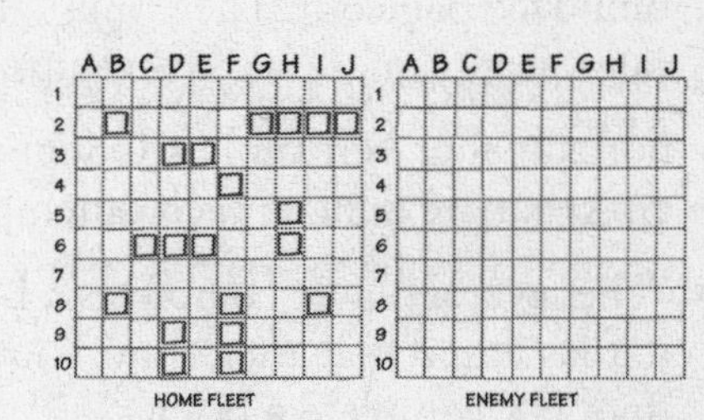

Game in progress: Player 1

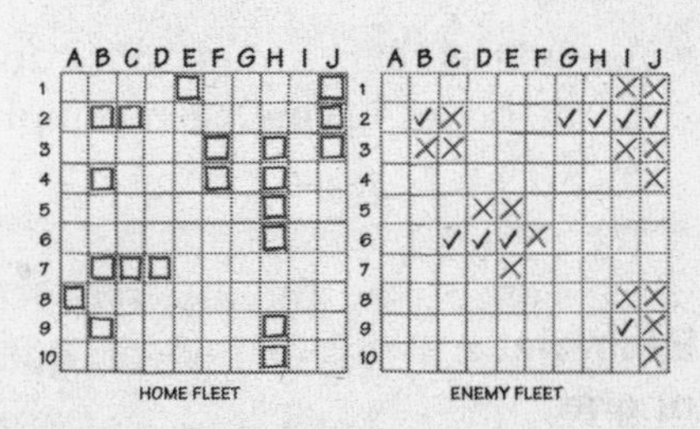

Game in progress: Player 2

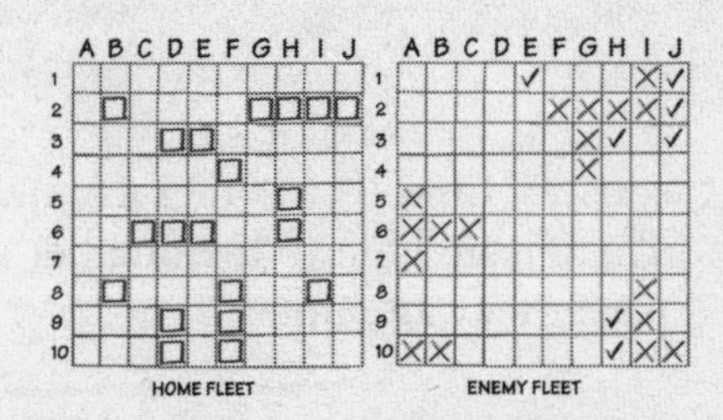

BOXES

Age 5+ **Players 2**

AIM

Players try to draw and initial as many boxes as they can.

PLAY

- Any number of dots is drawn on a piece of paper in rows. About ten rows by ten is a good number.
- Players take turns. In each turn they may draw a horizontal or vertical line to join up any two dots that are next to each other.
- Whenever a player completes a box, he or she initials it and may then draw another line that does not complete a box.
- As soon as there are no more dots to be joined – all the boxes having been completed – the game ends.

Example of grid

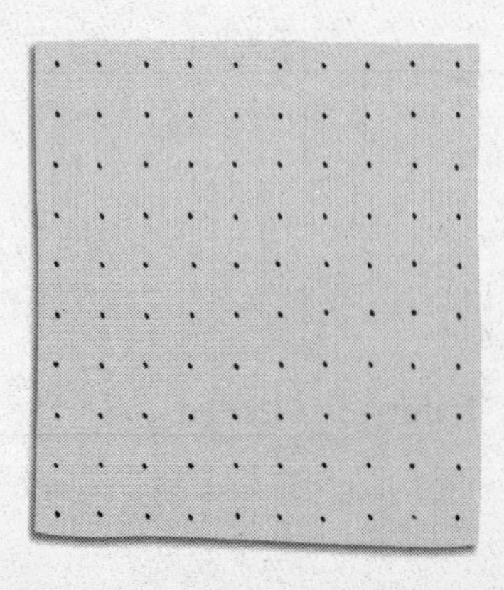

Game in progress

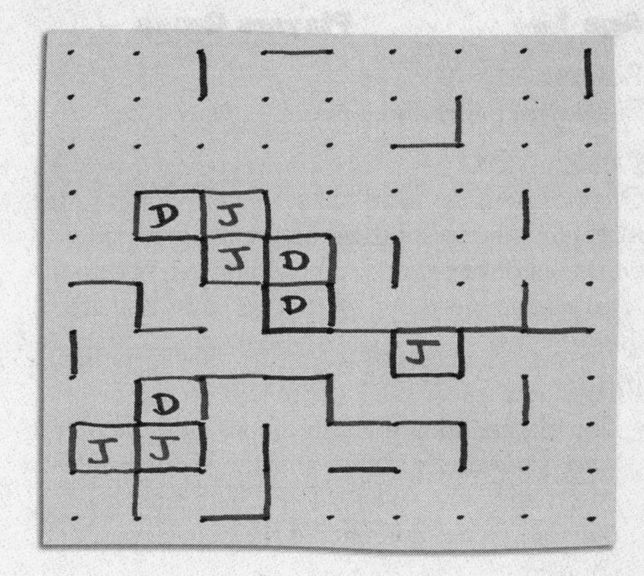

WINNING
The player with the highest number of initialled boxes is the winner.

VARIATION
Another way of playing is to try to form as few boxes as possible – the players join up as many dots as they can before being forced to complete a box. The winner is the player with the lowest number of initialled boxes.

MURDER IN THE DARK

Age 10+ **Players Group**

Equipment

Envelopes, paper and a pen.

Preparation

One person must hand out sealed envelopes to the players. Only two of them have anything written on the piece of paper inside. On one is written 'You are the murderer.' The other says 'You are the detective.'

Play

- The players open their envelopes, and the player who has been chosen to play the 'detective' lets everyone know of this. (The others must keep quiet about the contents of their envelopes, of course.)
- When all the players are ready, the detective turns out the lights for one minute.
- During this time, the players mill about in the dark and the 'murderer' commits the crime by *very gently* squeezing someone's neck.
- The moment the victim feels the murderer's hands, he or she must scream loudly and fall to the floor.
- Meanwhile, the 'murderer' must try to get as far away from the scene of the crime as possible in order to appear innocent.
- A few seconds after the scream, the detective

puts the lights back on, noting the positions of all the players.

- The detective asks the players questions about the 'murder'. They must all answer truthfully, except the murderer, who may lie as much as he or she likes.
- When the detective thinks he or she has deduced the identity of the murderer, he officially accuses someone.
- If the detective is correct, the murderer must confess. But if he is wrong (and he only gets one guess), the murderer wins and the mystery remains unsolved.

SCISSORS, PAPER, STONE

Age 10+ **Players 2**

This ancient game is also known as Hic, Haec, Hoc. Three objects (scissors, a piece of paper and a stone) are indicated by positions of the hand:

a) two fingers making a V shape represent scissors;

b) an open hand represents a piece of paper; and

c) a clenched fist represents a stone.

AIM

To guess correctly and to win the rounds.

PLAY

- Two players hide one hand behind their backs and adopt one of the three positions.
- One player calls 'One, two, three' (or 'Hic, haec, hoc') and as the third number or word is called the players show their hands.
- The winner of a round is decided with reference to the following statements: scissors can cut paper; paper may be wrapped around a stone; and a stone can blunt the scissors. Thus, if one player chooses scissors and the other player paper, the player who chooses scissors wins the round. If both players decide on the same object, the round is a draw. Players usually play a predetermined number of rounds.
- The winner is the player who wins the largest number of rounds.

Musical Games

LONDON BRIDGE

Age 3+ **Players Group**

PREPARATION

Two players are chosen to be the bridge. Each chooses to be either silver or gold.

PLAY

- The bridge is formed by the two players joining hands.
- The rest dance in a circle, passing under the bridge. On the word 'lady' the arms of the bridge come down and catch one of the dancers.
- They ask, 'What will you pay me, silver or gold?' Depending on the answer, the captured player stands behind one side of the bridge and the

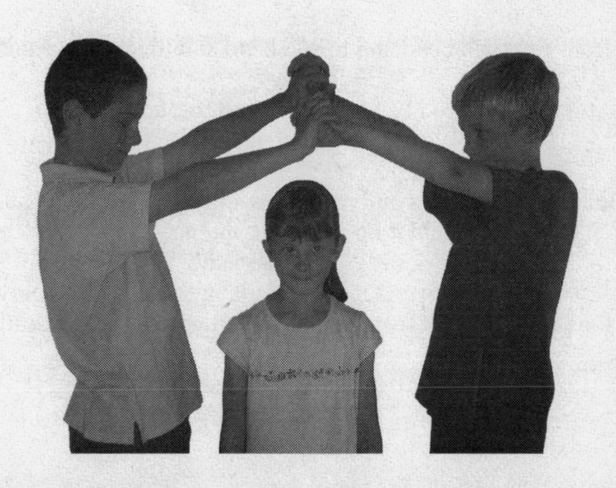

game goes on until all the dancers are caught. Often, the game ends with the two lines of players having a tug-of-war.

London Bridge is falling down, falling down, falling down,
London Bridge is falling down,
My fair lady.

Build it up with sticks and stones, sticks and stones, sticks and stones,
Build it up with sticks and stones,
My fair lady.

Sticks and stones will fall away, fall away, fall away,
Sticks and stones will fall away,
My fair lady.

Build it up with iron bars, iron bars, iron bars,
Build it up with iron bars,
My fair lady.

Irons bars will bend and break, bend and break, bend and break,
Iron bars will bend and break,
My fair lady.

Build it up with pins and nails, pins and nails, pins and nails,
Build it up with pins and nails,
My fair lady.

Pins and nails will rust and break, rust and break, rust and break,
Pins and nails will rust and break,
My fair lady.

OLD MACDONALD HAD A FARM

Age 3+ Players Group

PLAY

- The players form a circle, standing or sitting.
- As each verse is sung, they imitate the animal sounds, and repeat all the other noises of the previous verses, so that as the game proceeds it becomes very raucous and exciting. The game can be extended for several more verses to include, for instance, cats, pigs, frogs, horses, and so on.

Old MacDonald had a farm, ee-aye-ee-aye-o,
And on that farm he had some cows, ee-aye-ee-aye-o,
With a Moo-moo here, a Moo-moo there,
Here a Moo, there a Moo, everywhere a Moo-moo,
Old MacDonald had a farm, ee-aye-ee-aye-o.

Old MacDonald had a farm, ee-aye-ee-aye-o,
And on that farm he had some ducks, ee-aye-ee-aye-o,
With a Quack-quack here, a Quack-quack there,
Here a Quack, there a Quack, everywhere a Quack-quack,
With a Moo-moo here, a Moo-moo there,
Here a Moo, there a Moo, everywhere a Moo-moo,
Old MacDonald had a farm, ee-aye-ee-aye-o.

Old MacDonald had a farm, ee-aye-ee-aye-o,
And on that farm he had some sheep, ee-aye-ee-aye-o,
With a Baa-baa here, a Baa-baa there,
Here a Baa, there a Baa, everywhere a Baa-baa,
With a Quack-quack here, a Quack-quack there,
Here a Quack, there a Quack, everywhere a Quack-quack,
With a Moo-moo here, a Moo-moo there,
Here a Moo, there a Moo, everywhere a Moo-moo,
Old MacDonald had a farm, ee-aye-ee-aye-o.

Old MacDonald had a farm, ee-aye-ee-aye-o,
And on that farm he had some dogs, ee-aye-ee-aye-o,
With a Woof-woof here, a Woof-woof there,
Here a Woof, there a Woof, everywhere a Woof-woof,
With a Baa-baa here, a Baa-baa there,
Here a Baa, there a Baa, everywhere a Baa-baa,
With a Quack-quack here, a Quack-quack there,
Here a Quack, there a Quack, everywhere a Quack-quack,
With a Moo-moo here, a Moo-moo there,
Here a Moo, there a Moo, everywhere a Moo-moo,
Old MacDonald had a farm, ee-aye-ee-aye-o.

MUSICAL PATTERNS

Age 5+ **Players Teams**

Equipment

A cassette player, or a musical instrument such as a piano, is needed to provide the music.

Preparation

Arrange players into teams of equal numbers.

Play

- The music starts and the players march, or dance, around the room as they wish.
- The host calls out a shape and stops the music, whereupon the players rush to find their teammates and form the shape. The host should start with easy shapes, such as a circle and a square, and progress to more complicated ones, such as letters of the alphabet.
- One point may be awarded in each round for the team with the best shape. The team that scores the highest number of points wins.

MUSICAL CHAIRS

Age 5+ **Players Group**

Equipment

Chairs and something to play music on.

Preparation

Chairs are placed around the room in a large circle. There should be one chair fewer than the number of players.

Play

- The players stand in the circle and, when the music starts, all dance around.
- When the music stops, each player tries to sit on a seat. The player left without a seat is eliminated.
- One chair is then removed from the circle and the music is restarted.
- The last person to stay in the game is the winner.

MUSICAL STATUES

Age 3+

Players Group

This game is an enjoyable 'quiet' alternative to Musical Chairs.

Equipment

Something to play music on.

Play

- Players dance around the room to music. When the music stops, the players immediately stop dancing and stand as still as statues.
- Any player seen moving is out.
- The music is started again fairly quickly, and the game continues. Eliminated players can help to spot moving statues.
- The last player to remain is the winner.

PASS THE PARCEL

Age 5+ **Players Group**

PREPARATION

A small present is wrapped in layer after layer of paper. Each layer should be secured with thread, glue, or a rubber band. Music – to be started and stopped by someone not taking part in the game – is also needed.

PLAY

- Players sit in a circle and one of them holds the parcel. When the music starts, players pass the parcel around the circle to the right.
- When the music stops, whoever is holding the parcel unwraps one layer of wrapping. The music is then restarted and the parcel passed on again.
- The game continues until someone takes off the final wrapping and so wins the present.

Picture Games

BUTTERFLIES

Age 5+ **Players 2**

Equipment

You will need about six tubes of brightly coloured oil paints, scissors, and a piece of paper for each player. This game can be quite messy.

Preparation

Fold each piece of paper in two.

Play

- Get those taking part to squeeze blobs of three different colours of paint on one half of their piece of paper (**a**). They should try to put some blobs near to the crease.
- Each player should then fold the paper together, and open it out (**b**). The result should resemble a butterfly, which could be cut out.
- The results are judged and a prize awarded to the creator of the best 'butterfly'.

LIGHTS OUT!

Age 10+ **Players Group**

EQUIPMENT

A pencil and a piece of paper are needed for each player. A non-playing judge is also needed.

PLAY

- Make sure the players are sitting comfortably and then turn out the lights.
- Ask them to draw a lake.
- When they have all finished and expect you to turn the light back on, ask them to draw a boat on the lake.
- When this has been done to the best of their ability, ask them to draw a house on the shore.
- Again, wait until they have finished and then ask them to draw a man in the boat, a tree by the house, a fisherman by the shore, some clouds in the sky, and so on until the picture has a number of elements.
- At this point turn the lights back on.
- The winner will be whoever is judged to have created the most recognisable scene.

PICTURE CONSEQUENCES

Age 5+ **Players Group**

AIM

Players cooperate to produce a funny picture.

PLAY

- The players draw parts of an animal or a person dressed in funny clothing, according to choice. They start with the head, then fold the paper so only the neck is showing.
- Each person passes the paper to his or her neighbour, who draws the next section, and so on.
- After drawing the feet, players may write down the name of the person whom they want the figure to represent!
- There is no winner, the game is played for fun.

Racing Games

ASSAULT COURSE

Age 5+ **Players Teams**

Equipment

Lots of obstacles and varied items are needed for the course – dressing-up clothes, sacks, balls, balloons, potatoes and spoons, for example.

Preparation

The objects are laid out in advance by the host along a course. Starting and finishing lines should be marked with string or chalk. Examples of possible obstacles include a long jump, a potato and spoon dash, a box to be leapt over, a rope for six skips, a sack for jumping in to the next obstacle, and an old shirt to put on.

Play

- The host first explains what has to be done at each point along the course. The object is for each team to complete the course.
- On the word 'Go!' the first member of each team runs the course and must cope with every obstacle in turn, as instructed.
- Once he or she has completed the course and reaches the finishing line, the next team member can start.
- The team with all its members at the finishing line first wins.

EGG-CUP RACE

Age 10+ **Players Teams**

Equipment
Two egg cups and a table-tennis ball are needed for each team. The egg cups should not be so large that a table-tennis ball, when placed in one, cannot be blown out.

Preparation
Players are separated into two teams. They sit on opposite sides of a table.

Play
- After 'Go!' the first player in each team takes the egg cups and puts the table-tennis ball in the first egg-cup. The idea is to blow the ball into the next egg cup, which can be as close as the players wish to the first one.
- When this is achieved, table-tennis ball and egg cups are passed on to the next member of the team, who has to do the same.
- The first team in which everyone has managed to blow the table-tennis ball into the second egg cup is the winner.

GOING AWAY

Age 5+ **Players Teams**

EQUIPMENT

Two suitcases packed with old clothes. One will be full of female clothes and objects; the other full of male clothes and items.

PREPARATION

The players are arranged into two equal teams – one of males and one of females. The teams stand as far away from the suitcases as possible.

PLAY

- When they are told to start, the first player from each team hops to the suitcase containing male items if the player is female – or a case containing female items if the player is male.
- The players put on the clothes and, if there is any make-up, or wigs or toiletries, they should attempt to utilise these in some way. Each then picks up the suitcase and hops back to the starting line. Once there, they remove the clothes and replace them in the cases.
- They now hop back to the end of the room with the cases, drop them and run back to the start. The next player performs the same routine.
- The first team to complete the course wins.

PASSING THE ORANGE

Age 5+

Players Teams

Aim

Seated players try to pass an orange down the line using their chins, or (in an alternative version) by using their feet!

Play

- Players divide into teams and stand in a line beside their leaders. Each leader is given an orange which is tucked between chin and chest. On the word 'Go!' he passes the orange to the next player – neither player may use his hands. (Alternatively, the players sit side-by-side in a line on the floor and the leader, legs together, cradles the orange on his feet. He then passes it to the feet of the next player.)
- The orange is passed from player to player. If the orange drops on the floor, or if a player uses his hands, the orange is returned to the leader to start again.
- The first team to pass the orange down the line wins.

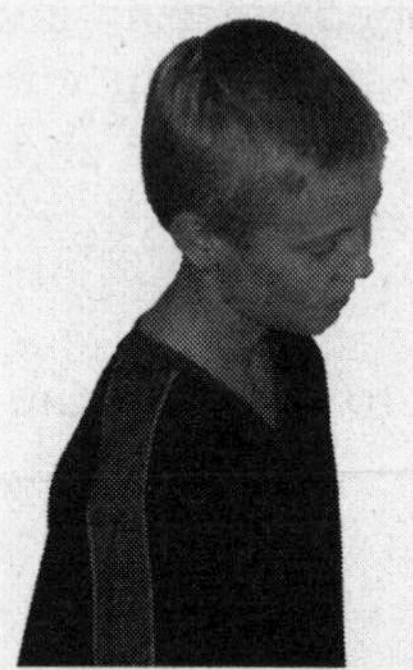

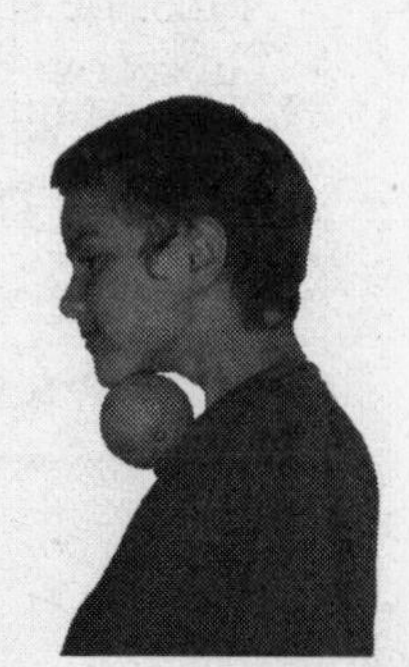

POTATO RACE

Age 5+ **Players Group**

EQUIPMENT

Five potatoes, two plates and one spoon are needed for each player.

PREPARATION

For each player, place a spoon on a plate at the starting line. Place another plate, holding five potatoes, on a line a few metres away.

PLAY

- On the word 'Go!' each player has to pick up a spoon, run to the plate containing the potatoes and – using only the spoon – scoop up the first potato. Each now runs back to the starting line and deposits the potato on the plate there.
- This procedure continues until all five potatoes have been successfully carried to the plate at the starting line.
- Players must only use one hand to carry the spoon. If a potato drops onto the ground, it must be scooped up again into the spoon.
- The winner is the first player to transport all their potatoes from one plate to the other.

Dice Games

BEETLE

Age 8+ **Players 2**

EQUIPMENT

1) One die, either an ordinary one or a special 'beetle die' marked B (body), H (head), L (legs), E (eye), F (feeler) and T (tail);

2) a simple drawing of a beetle as a guide, showing its various parts and (when an ordinary die is used) their corresponding numbers (1=B; 2=H; 3=L; 4=E; 5=F; 6=T);

3) a pencil and a piece of paper for each player.

AIM

Each player, by throwing the die, tries to complete his drawing of the beetle.

PLAY

- Each player throws the die once only in each round. Each player must begin by throwing a B (or a 1); this permits the player to draw the body.
- When this has been drawn, he or she can throw for other parts of the beetle that can be joined to the body. An H or a 2 must be thrown to link the head to the body before the feelers (F or 5) and eyes (E or 4) can be added.
- Each eye or feeler requires its own throw. A throw of L or 3 permits the player to add three legs to one side of the body.

- A further throw of L or 3 is necessary for the other three legs. Sometimes it is agreed that a player may continue to throw during a turn for as long as he or she throws parts of the body that can be used.

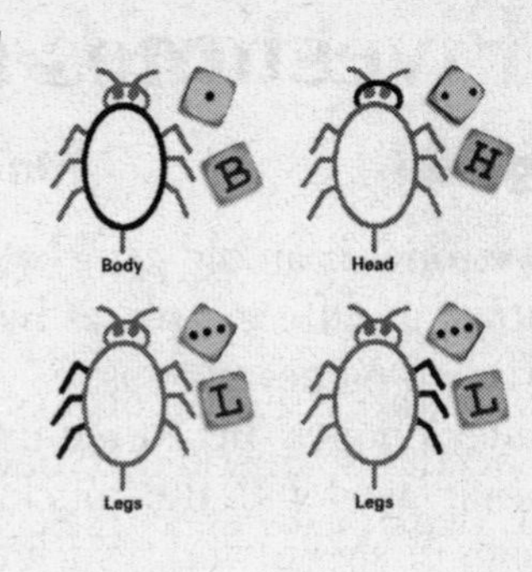

- The first to complete his or her beetle scores 13 points and is the winner. The 13 points represent the total of each part of the beetle (body, head, tail, two feelers, two eyes and six legs).

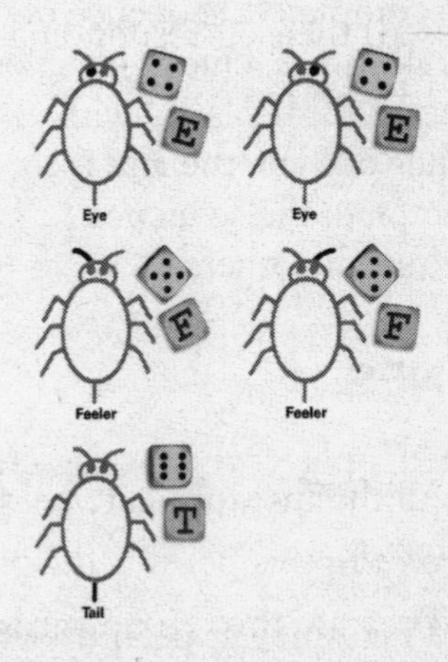

CONTINUING PLAY

When a series of games is played, each player counts one point for every part of the beetle he or she has been able to draw, and cumulative scores are carried from round to round. The winner is the player with the highest score at the end of the series or the first to reach a previously agreed total score.

Fivestones and Jacks

Age 8+ **Players 2**

Fivestones is an old game, known in different places by different names such as Knucklebones (because it used to be played with the knucklebones of sheep) and Chuckies.

Aim

To complete a sequence of small games, chiefly using only one hand. If played with other players, the aim is to complete the sequence before the others.

ONES

Play

- All the fivestones are held in the palm of one hand.
- They are thrown upwards; while they are in the air the hand is turned over and the player tries to catch the fivestones on the back of the hand. If successful, he or she moves on to the next game of Twos. If the player catches only some of the stones, he or she puts all but one on the floor, throws the remaining one in the air and tries to pick the rest up one by one with the throwing hand before catching the one in the air

with the same hand. The stones can be transferred to the free hand.

TWOS

PLAY

- Four of the fivestones are scattered on the floor.
- The remaining one is thrown in the air and the player tries to pick up two of the four with the throwing hand in time to catch the one in the air with the same hand.
- If successful, he or she throws again to pick up the remaining pair. Beginners are allowed to use their throw to nudge the scattered fivestones closer together. Experts must pick them up where they lie.

THREES

PLAY

- Four fivestones are scattered on the floor.
- The remaining one is thrown, and the player picks up one from the ground.
- He or she throws again and picks up the remaining three, all with the throwing hand.

FOURS

PLAY

- Played like Twos and Threes, but all four scattered fivestones must be picked up at once.

BUSHELS

PLAY

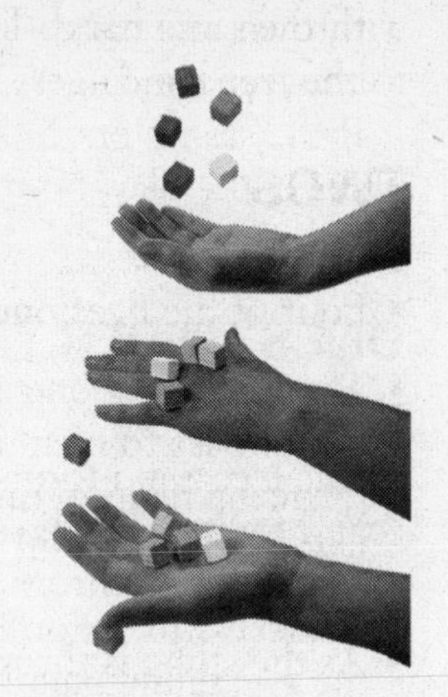

- The fivestones are thrown up (picture **1**) and caught on the back of the hand (picture **2**), thrown again and caught in the palm.
- Any not caught are then picked up one by one (picture **3**), but none of the stones may be transferred to the free hand.

CLAWS

PLAY

- The fivestones are thrown and caught on the back of the hand.
- If all are caught they are thrown again and caught in the palm.

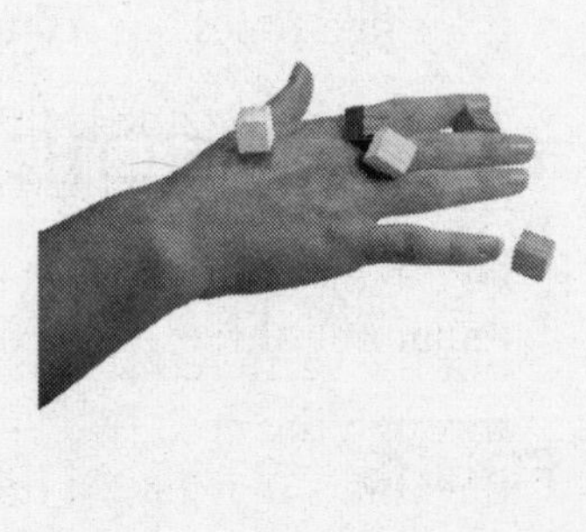

- If some are dropped, the caught ones are dropped, the caught ones are kept on the back of the hand, and the others are picked up between the fingers or finger and thumb.
- Then the stones on the back of the hand are

thrown and caught in the palm, and the stones between the fingers manoeuvred into the palm. If the stones on the back of the hand fall at any stage, the player must begin again.

ONES UNDER THE ARCH

PLAY

- The free hand forms an arch with the thumb and forefinger. The stones are scattered and one picked up to throw.
- As the stone is thrown, one of the scattered stones is knocked through the arch with the throwing hand before the stone in the air is caught.
- This is repeated until all the stones are through the arch. Beginners can take a throw to manoeuvre the stone before knocking it through the arch.

TWOS UNDER THE ARCH

PLAY

- The game proceeds as Ones Under the Arch, but the scattered stones must be pushed through the arch two at a time. As before, beginners may take a throw to manoeuvre the scattered stones before knocking them through.

VARIATION

In the style of Twos Under the Arch, play Threes Under the Arch and Fours Under the Arch.

SWEEP THE FLOOR

PLAY

- This is a sequence of actions, accompanied by spoken words. The stones, except for one throwing stone, are scattered.
- First, the stone is thrown and the throwing hand wipes the table as the player says, 'Sweep the floor!'
- Second, one of the scattered stones is moved as the player says, 'Move the chair!'
- Third, the 'chair' is picked up and the player says 'Pick it up!'
- Last, the chair is put back on the table or ground again, 'Put it down!'
- In the second round, all these actions are repeated, but the table receives two wipes, and two chairs are moved, picked up and put down.
- In the third round everything is done in threes, and in threes, and in the fourth, by fours.

Players who make any mistakes return to the beginning of that round.

BIG BEN

PLAY

- A tower is built of four of the fivestones.
- The remaining stone is thrown and the topmost stone from the tower is removed and placed in the non-throwing hand. If the tower topples, it

must be rebuilt and the game started again.

- The game continues until the tower has been dismantled.
- When the last stone is picked up, the throwing stone should be caught in the non-throwing hand, so that all the stones are together in that hand.
- The game can also be played in reverse, the four stones held in the non-throwing hand, and each stone placed on top of the next in throws.

JACKS

Nearly all of the games for fivestones can also be played with jacks and a rubber ball. There are five jacks. Only the ball is thrown, and is allowed one bounce before being caught.

Spellicans

Age 5+ **Players 2**

This game, which originated in China, is also called Spillikins. Players try their skill at removing straws or small sticks from a pile, one at a time and without disturbing any of their neighbours. Any number of players can take part.

Equipment

Spellicans is played with a set of about 30 thin strips of wood or plastic. These strips, called spellicans, have carved heads representing animals, people, etc. There is also a carved hook for moving the strips.

Start of play

The order of play is determined by the throw of a die or some other means. The last person in the playing order then takes all the spellicans in one hand and drops them onto the table or floor. He must not interfere with any spellican after it has left his hand.

Play

- At his or her turn, each player attempts to use the carved hook to remove a spellican from the pile without disturbing any of the others. Once a player has started moving a particular spellican, they cannot transfer to a different one.
- If the player successfully removes a spellican from the pile, he or she keeps it and tries to

remove another spellican from the pile. A player's turn continues until a spellican other than the one being attacked is disturbed.

- Play continues in this way until all the spellicans have been taken.
- Each spellican has a points value, and a game is won by the player with the highest score. Spellicans that are generally fairly easy to move have a low value, and more elaborate and difficult to move spellicans have a correspondingly higher value.

VARIATION

The game is similar to Jackstraws (also known as Jerkstraws, Juggling Sticks and Pick-a-stick). This is played with about 50 wood or plastic sticks or straws, about 15 cm (6 in) long, rounded and with pointed ends, and they are coloured according to their point value. Players remove the sticks with their fingers or, in some versions of the game, may use a stick of a specified colour after they have drawn one from the pile.

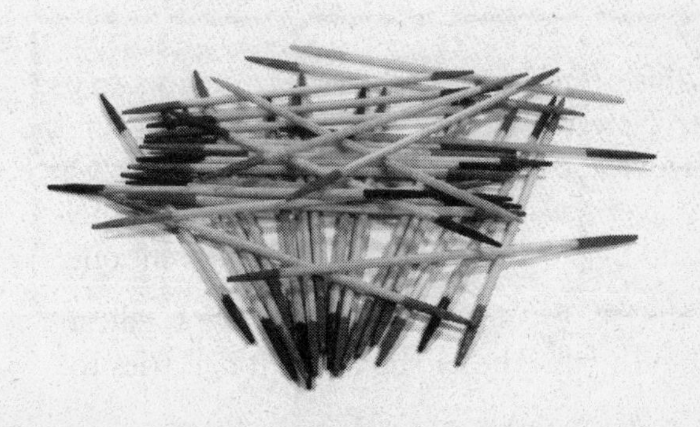

SQUAYLES

Age 5–10 **Players 2**

PREPARATION

As with the other matchstick games, the matches should be struck and extinguished before being used. Any number of matches are arranged in a pattern of squares.

AIM

To be able to pick up the last match.

PLAY

- The players take turns to pick up matches. They may take one or two at a time, provided the two are next to each other, though they do not have to be in a straight line.
- The winner is the player who picks up the last match.

Start of play

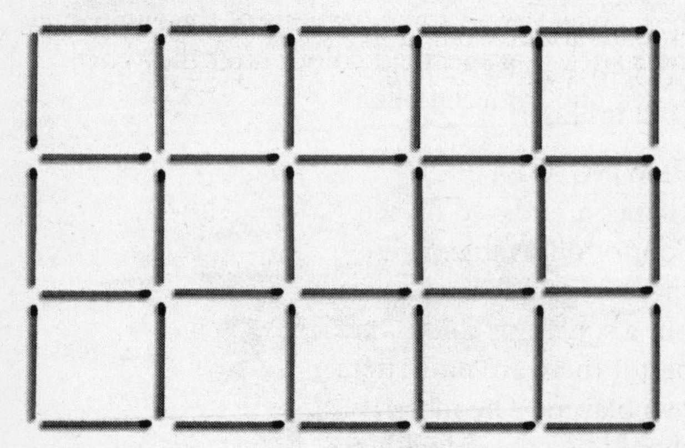

Tiddlywinks

Age 5+ **Players 2**

In the standard game of Tiddlywinks, each player attempts to put small discs or 'winks' into a cup by shooting them with a larger disc called a 'shooter'. Variations include games based on sports such as tennis and golf.

Equipment

Each player usually has a shooter and four winks. A target cup is also needed. Winks and shooters must be slightly pliable and are commonly made of bone or plastic. Winks are usually about 1.5 cm (about 0.5 in) and shooters about 2.5 cm (1 in) in diameter. Each player's winks and shooters should be of a different colour.

Target cups are made of plastic, wood, or glass and are about 4 cm (1.5 in) across and 2.5–5 cm (1–2 in) high.

shooters

Playing area

Games are played on the floor or on a table. Any shape of table may be used but a square or round one is best if there are more than two players. The table should be covered with a thick cloth or piece of felt.

winks

STANDARD TIDDLYWINKS

SHOOTING

A player shoots a wink by stroking and then pressing the edge of the shooter against the top edge of the wink and so making the wink jump into the air. A wink is shot from where it lies after the previous turn.

PLAY

- The cup is placed in the centre of the playing area, and each player places his or her winks in a line in front of him.
- Order of play is often decided by a preliminary shot – first shot of the game going to the player who gets his or her wink nearest the cup.
- Play is then usually clockwise. Each player shoots one wink in a turn plus one extra shot each time he or she gets a wink into the cup. Any wink that is partly covered by another is out of play. A player whose wink is covered by an opponent's wink must either wait until the opponent moves his or her wink or must attempt to remove the opponent's wink by hitting it with one of his or her own winks. Any wink that stops against the side of the cup is out of play until it is knocked level onto the table by another wink. A wink that is shot off the table does not go out of play. It must be replaced on the table at the point where it went off.
- Tiddlywinks may be scored in two ways:
  a) players count the number of games they win;

b) players score one point for each wink in the cup.

- The game is won by the first player to get all his or her tiddlywinks in the cup.

TIDDLYWINKS TENNIS

Preparation

The lines of a tennis court should be marked on the floor or the tiddlywinks cloth. (Dimensions for the court should be varied to suit the skill of the players and the height of the net.) An improvised net can be made with folded paper or card, or with a row of books.

Play

- Players shoot a wink back and forth over the net, gaining points whenever their opponents fail to get the wink over the net or shoot it so that it goes outside the limits of the court. The game can be played by two players (singles) or four players (doubles). In the doubles version, partners take alternate turns to shoot the wink from their side of the net. Rules for service can be modified to suit the skill of the players – e.g. extra shots allowed to get the wink over the net or no restrictions on where in the opponent's court the wink must land.

- A match is scored in games and sets as in tennis, with the first to win three sets taking the match.

Spoken Word Games

ANIMAL, VEGETABLE OR MINERAL

Age 5–10 **Players Group**

Sometimes called Twenty Questions, this game is one of the oldest and most familiar word-guessing games.

Aim

Players try to guess an object thought of by one of the others.

Play

- One of the players thinks of an object. It may be general (e.g. 'a ship'), specific (e.g. 'the Lusitania'), or a feature (e.g. 'the bridge of the Lusitania').
- He or she then tells the others the composition of his chosen object (i.e. animal, vegetable or mineral). The three categories may be defined as follows:

  1) animal: all forms of animal life or anything of animal origin, e.g. a centipede, a tortoiseshell button;

  2) vegetable: all forms of vegetable life or anything of vegetable origin, e.g. a wooden cotton reel, a carrot;

  3) mineral: anything inorganic or of inorganic origin, e.g. glass, a car. Objects are often a

combination of categories, for example, a can of beer or a leather shoe.

- The other players then ask up to 20 questions to try to guess the object. They should ask questions of a general nature rather than make random guesses, until they feel confident that they are near to knowing the object.
- As each question is put to the player, he or she must reply either 'Yes' or 'No', or 'I don't know', as appropriate.
- The first player to guess the object correctly may choose an object for a new round of play. If no one has guessed the object by the time 20 questions have been asked, the players are told what it was, and the same person – or, if two teams are playing, a person in the other team – may choose an object for the next round.

BUZZ

Age 10+ **Players Group**

This game should be played as briskly as possible for maximum enjoyment.

Aim

To count numbers remembering which ones to replace with the word 'Buzz'.

Play

- The players sit in a circle.
- One player calls out 'One', the next player 'Two', the next 'Three', and so on.

- As soon as the number five, or any multiple of five, is reached, the players must say 'Buzz'. If the number contains a five but is not a multiple of five, only part of it is replaced by buzz. (For example, 52 would be 'Buzz two'.) If a player forgets to say 'Buzz' or hesitates too long, he or she drops out.
- The last player remaining in the game is the winner.

VARIATIONS

A variation is called Fizz. This is played exactly like Buzz, except that players say 'Fizz' for seven or multiples of seven. Another variation, Buzz-Fizz, combines the two games, so that 57, for example, becomes Buzz-Fizz.

GHOSTS

Age 10+ **Players Group**

AIM

Players take it in turns to contribute a letter to an unstated word while trying to avoid completing any word.

PLAY

- The first player begins by thinking of any word (e.g. rabbit) and calls out the first letter (R).
- The next player then thinks of a word beginning with R (e.g. rescue) and calls out its second letter (E).

- Play then continues in this way until one of the players is unable to contribute a letter that does not complete a word.
- Whenever a player completes a word – and the other players notice – that player loses a 'life'. This is true even if the word is completed by accident and the player was thinking of another word.
- If a player is unable to think of a suitable word, they may try to bluff their way out of the situation by calling out a letter of an imaginary word.
- If, however, they hesitate for too long or the other players suspect that they have no particular word in mind, they may challenge the player. The challenged player must state the word and if they cannot do so lose a life. If the explanation is satisfactory, however, the challenger loses a life. Whenever a player loses a first life they becomes 'a third of a ghost'. Losing a second life makes them 'two-thirds of a ghost', and if a player loses a third life they become a whole ghost and must drop out of the game.

- The game is won by the player who manages to survive the longest.

I WENT ON A TRIP

Age 10+ **Players Group**

AIM

Players try to remember and repeat a growing list of items.

PLAY

- One of the players chooses an article – for example an umbrella – and says, 'I went on a trip and took my umbrella.'
- The next player repeats that sentence and adds a second item after 'umbrella'. In this way the players gradually build up a list of articles.
- Each time his or her turn comes, a player repeats the list and adds another item. When a player cannot repeat the list correctly, the list is closed and the next player in the group begins a new list.

VARIATION

A variation known as City of Boston is very similar to I Went on a Trip, but players must add to a list of items for sale. Thus the first player might say 'I shall sell you a bunch of violets when you come to the City of Boston'. The other players then repeat that sentence in turn and add an item that he or she will sell.

ONE MINUTE, PLEASE

Age 10+ **Players Group**

Aim

To speak for one minute on a given topic.

Play

- One player is chosen as timekeeper and also picks topics for each player to talk about.
- When it is his or her turn to speak, a player is told his or her topic. This may be anything from a serious topic such as 'The current political situation' to something frivolous like 'Why women wear hats'. Players may choose to treat the subject in any manner they please and what they say may be utter nonsense, provided they do not deviate from the topic, hesitate unduly or repeat themselves.
- Other players may challenge the speaker if they feel he or she has broken a rule. If the time-keeper agrees, then the speaker must drop out and the next player is given a new topic.
- The winner is the player who manages to speak for an entire minute. If, however, two or more players achieve this, the others decide which of the speeches was the best, or alternatively further rounds may be played.

TABOO

Age 10+ **Players Group**

AIM

Players try to avoid saying a particular letter of the alphabet.

PLAY

- One player is the questioner and chooses which letter is to be 'taboo'.
- He or she then asks each of the players in turn any question he or she likes.
- Players must answer with a sensible phrase or sentence that does not contain the forbidden letter – if they do use the taboo letter, they are out.
- The last player to stay in the game wins and becomes the next questioner.

Example

F is TABOO

Questioner: 'Name a ball game'

Player 1 'Cricket' STAYS IN

Player 2 'Basketball' STAYS IN

Player 3 'GolF' GOES OUT

WORD ASSOCIATION

Age 10+ **Players Group**

PLAY

- Players stand in a circle.
- The first player says the first word that enters his or her head.
- The player to the left has to respond immediately with a word that is somehow linked to the first word – for example, cup = tea = bag = paper, etc. A non-player acts as judge. Players hesitating too long before replying are eliminated. A player may be asked to explain the association between words if his or her reply does not seem to be linked to the previous word.
- The last player left in the game is the winner.

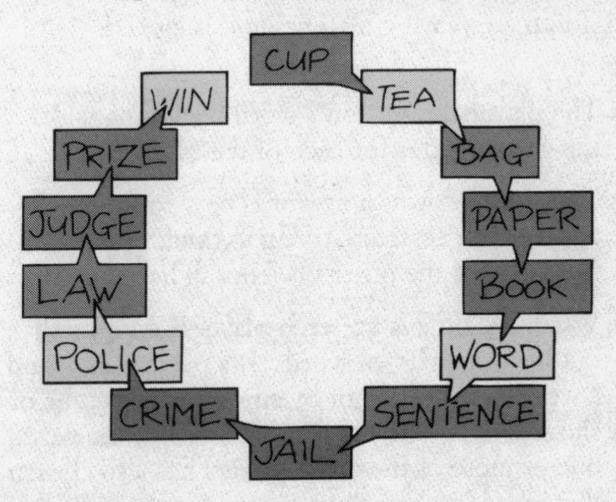

Pen and Paper Games

CATEGORIES

Age 10+ **Players Group**

AIM

Players try to think of words or names within particular categories beginning with particular letters.

PREPARATION

Each player is given pencil and paper. The players decide on between six and a dozen different categories; these may be easy ones for children (e.g. animals, colours) or more difficult for any adults who are also playing (e.g. rivers, chemicals). Each player lists the categories on his or her paper. One of the players chooses any letter of the alphabet – preferably an 'easy' letter such as 'a' or 'd' if young children are playing. A time limit is agreed.

PLAY

- The players try to find a word beginning with the chosen letter for each of the categories.
- They write down their words next to the appropriate category, trying to think of words that none of the other players will have chosen.
- When the time is up, each player in turn reads out his or her list of words. If a player has found a word not thought of by any other player, he or she scores two points for that word. If, however, one or more of the other players has also chosen that word, each of them scores one point. If the

player could not find a word at all, or if his or her choice of word did not correctly fit the category, he or she gets no points. (Disagreement about the relevance of a word to a category must be resolved by a vote among the other players.)

- The winner is the player with the highest score for their list of words. Any number of rounds may be played, using either the same or different categories; the chosen letter, however, must be different for each round. Players may take it in turns to choose a letter at the start of a round. Players make a note of their scores at the end of each round. The winner is the player with the highest points total at the end of the final round.

VARIATION

In a variation, known as Guggenheim, the players choose a keyword of about four to six letters, for example, 'person'. The letters of the keyword are spaced out, and players try to find words for each of the categories beginning with each of the letters of the keyword.

	Place	Plant	Colour	Food	Wood	Name
P	Peru	poppy	pink	plum	pine	Peter
E	Eire	endive	ecru	egg	elm	Edward
R	Rome	reed	red	ragout	redwood	Robin
S	Seoul	soya	sepia	soup	sycamore	Sally
O	Ohio	orpine	ochre	orange	oak	Oliver
N	New York	nemesia	navy	noodles	nutmeg-tree	Nicola

EMERGENCY CONSEQUENCES

Age 10+ **Players Group**

EQUIPMENT

Pencil and paper for each player.

PLAY

- Each player has to think of an 'emergency' and phrase it in the form of a question, for example: 'What would you do if your television exploded and the curtains caught fire?'
- The paper is then folded in half so the question is not visible and handed to the player on the left.
- The next player now writes down what he would do in an emergency (not knowing, of course, what the first player wrote) and the results are read out. For example, the second player might respond: 'I would boil the kettle and call a vet.'
- This game is for amusement only.

What would you do if your father fell down the stairs and broke his leg?

I would set the dog on him and call the police

FAIR AND SQUARE

Age 10+

Players Group

Equipment

Pencil and paper for each player.

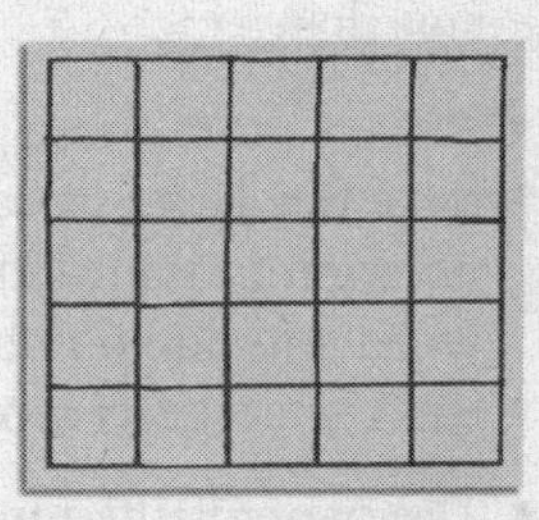

Preparation

Players must draw a large square on a piece of paper and divide it into 25 smaller squares by drawing four vertical, and four horizontal, lines within the outline.

Play

- One player is chosen to start and calls out a letter of the alphabet. All the players must put the letter in one of their squares.

- When this is done, the next player chooses a letter and the players decide where to place it in their grids. Players may choose the same letter more than once.

- The game continues until all 25 squares are filled. The idea is to arrange your letters so that your grid contains a number of words of three or more letters. Words can run up and down. Players may, of course, choose letters to suit their

- Players score three points for a five-letter word, two points for a four-letter word and one point for each three-letter word.
- The winner is the person with the highest score. For example, this player's final score is 19 points, as shown below.

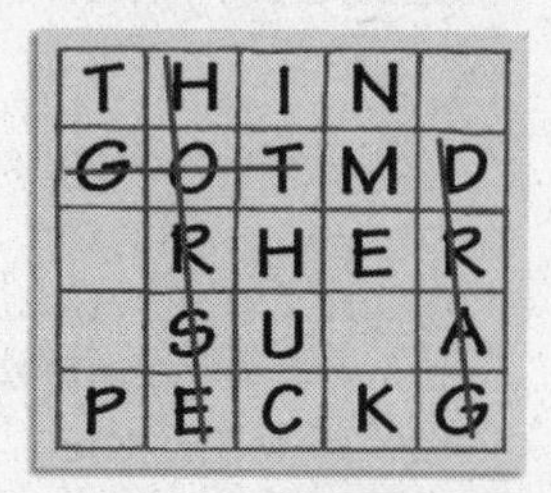

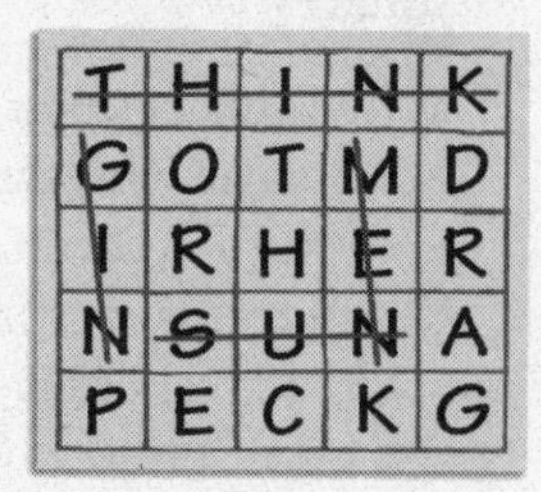

Calculating the score

THINK, HORSE: 3 points each = 6 points.

DRAG, PECK, THIN: 2 points each = 6 points.

INK, GOT, HER, SUN, GIN, MEN, RAG:
1 point each = 7 points.

Total: 19 points

HANGMAN

Age 10+ **Players 2**

AIM

Players try to guess a secret word.

PLAY

- One person thinks of a word of about five or six letters.
- This player writes down the same number of dashes as there are letters in his or her word.
- The other players then start guessing the letters in the word, calling out one letter at a time.
- If the guess is a successful one, the letter is written by the first player above the appropriate dash – if it appears more than once in a word it must be entered as often as it occurs.
- If the guess is an incorrect one, however, the first player may start to draw a hanged man – one line of the drawing representing each wrong letter. The other players must try to guess the secret word before the first player can complete the drawing of the hanged man.
- If one player guesses the word, he or she may take a turn at choosing a word. If the hanged man is completed before the word is guessed, the same player may choose again. To make the game more difficult, longer words can be chosen, or a group of words making a phrase or the title of a book or film though with a clue as to the category.

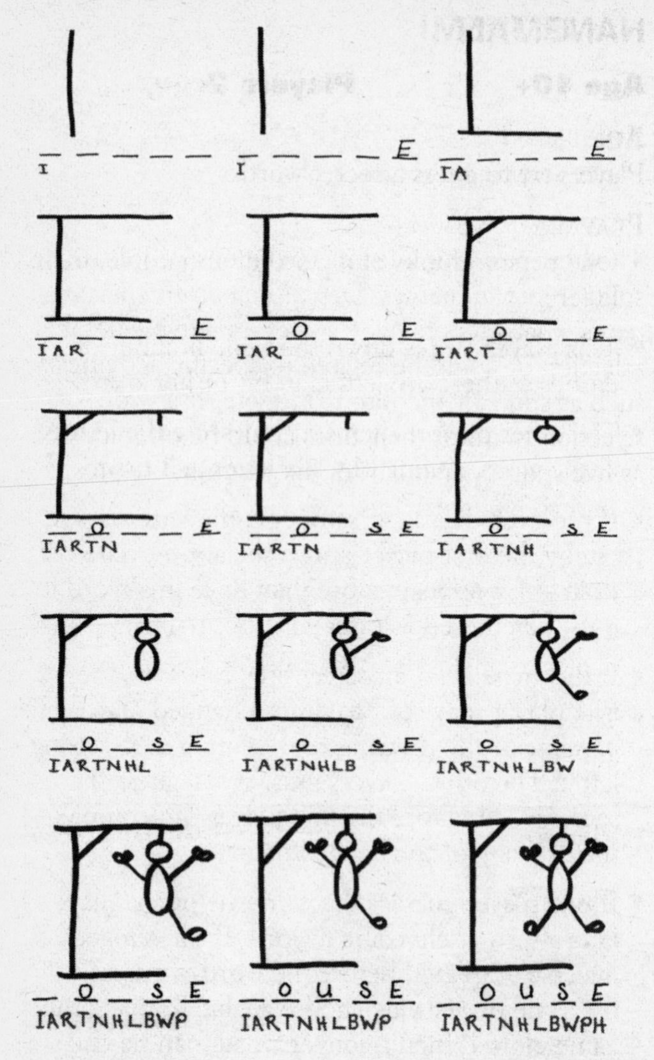

- In this game the word was 'mouse', but the hangman was completed before it was guessed.

NAME THEM!

Age 10+ **Players Group**

Equipment

Paper and pencil for each player.

Preparation

The host prepares a list of 20 famous people, then splits it into 40 names. Depending on the participants, characters may be a wide-ranging general selection or could be related to specific activities such as sport or the film world, etc. If a wide selection is given, then clues could be offered such as five sports personalities, six historical figures, two film characters, etc.

Play

- Players have 10 minutes to write down which surnames they think match up with which first names to create the names of 20 famous people.
- The player with the highest number of correct answers is the winner.

1. David	6. George
2. Robbie	7. Julia
3. Kylie	8. Zidane
4. Brad	9. Michael
5. Bill	10. Carey

11. Tony
12. Bart
13. Sampras
14. Owen
15. Jim
16. Jones
17. Pitt
18. Mouse
19. Williams
20. Marion
21. Tim
22. Ronan
23. Pete
24. Aniston
25. Steve
26. Jennifer
27. Clinton
28. Mickey
29. Minogue
30. Nelson
31. Roberts
32. Redgrave
33. ZInedine
34. Blair
35. Keating
36. Bush
37. Mandela
38. Beckham
39. Henman
40. Simpson

SCAFFOLD

Age 10+ **Players Group**

EQUIPMENT

A dictionary, and paper and pencil for each player.

PLAY

- Players are given three letters (at least one of which should be a vowel), and 10 minutes to write down words that contain all three letters. Words must be of four letters or more. Plurals are not allowed.

  For example, if the letters are A, M, T, the list of words may include: TEAM, MATE, MEAT, MATADOR, TRAMP, TOMATO, MATCH, ATTEMPT, MATTER . . .

- The player with the highest number of correct words will be the winner.

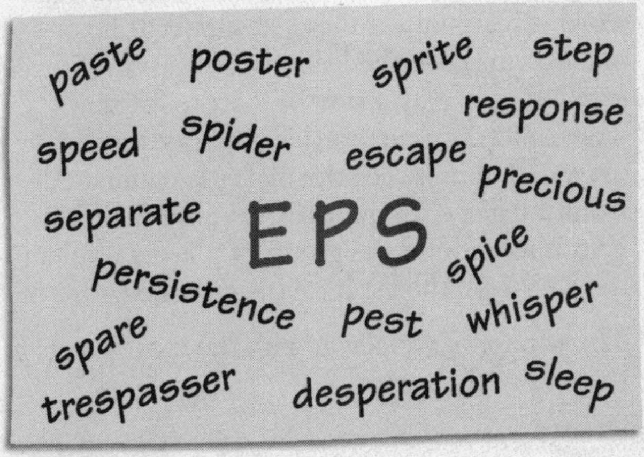

paste poster sprite step
response
speed spider escape precious
separate EPS
persistence spice
spare pest whisper
trespasser desperation sleep

SPELLING BEE

Age 7+ **Players Group**

Aim

To spell as many words as possible correctly, so gaining the maximum number of points.

Preparation

One person is chosen as leader, and the other players sit facing him or her. The leader may be given a previously prepared list of words or may make one up. It is a good idea to have a dictionary to hand in case of disputes.

Play

- The leader then reads out the first word on the list and the first player tries to spell it.
- The player is allowed 10 seconds in which to make an attempt at the correct spelling. If he or she succeeds, one point is scored and the next word is read out for the next player. If he or she makes a mistake, the leader reads out the correct spelling. The player does not score for that word, and the next word is read out for the next player. (Alternatively, the player is eliminated from the game for an incorrect answer.) Play continues around the group of players until all the words on the list have been spelled.
- The winner is the player with the most points at the end of the game.

BACKWARDS SPELLING BEE

Age 7+ **Players Group**

In Backwards Spelling Bee, a more difficult version of the game, players must spell their words backwards. Scoring is the same as in the standard game.

VARIATION

For Right or Wrong Spelling Bee, the players should form two teams, and line up opposite each other.

PLAY

- The leader calls out a word to each player in turn, alternating between teams.
- Each time a player spells a word, the player standing opposite him must call out 'Right' or 'Wrong'.
- If he calls a correctly spelled word wrong or a misspelled word right, he is eliminated from the game and must leave the line. (Players may move around once their numbers have been depleted, so that there is a caller for each player in the other team.)
- If the caller makes a correct call, he gets the next word to spell.
- The last team to retain any players wins.

SURPRISE SENTENCES

Age 7+ **Players Teams**

AIM

Each team tries to write a sentence, with each player in the team writing one word of it.

PREPARATION

For each team, a large sheet of paper is attached to a wall or to a board propped upright.

PLAY

- Each team lines up opposite its sheet of paper and the leader is given a pencil.
- At the word 'Go!' the leader runs up to his or her team's paper and writes any word he or she likes and then runs back to the team, hands the pencil to the next player and goes to the end of the team.
- As soon as the next player gets the pencil, he or she goes to the paper and adds a second word either in front of, or behind, the leader's word.
- Play continues in this way with each player adding one word. The words should be chosen and put together so that they can be part of a grammatically correct sentence.
- Each player, except the last, must avoid completing the sentence. The last player should be able to complete the sentence by adding just one word and he or she also puts in the punctuation.

- Players may not confer and choose a sentence before writing their words.
- The first team to construct a sentence with one word from each player wins the game.

WHAT'S NEXT?

Age 10+ **Players Group**

Equipment

Paper and pencil for each player.

Preparation

The host prepares a number of 'progressions' in advance. These can be numerical or alphabetical. Examples are:

What is the next number in this sequence? 5 6 8 11... (Answer: 15).

What is the next letter in this sequence? A E I M... (Answer: Q).

In the first example, you add one to five to make six, then add two to six to make eight, and add three to eight to make eleven. To continue the sequence, therefore, you must add four to eleven to make fifteen. Likewise, in the second example, there are three letters missing between each entry in the sequence.

Play

- The players are allowed 3 minutes or so to work out what letter or number comes next in each progression.
- The winner is the player with the most correct answers.

Answers to sequences opposite are:
128; IR; 28; T; 32; J; 85; 34; 4,294,967,296.

1 2 4 8 16 32 64 ....

MN LO KP JQ ....

1 2 3 4 6 9 13 19 ....

Z B X D V F ....

31 28 31 30 31 ....

J F M A M J ....

5 9 13 21 33 53 ....

1 1 2 3 5 8 13 21 ....

2 4 16 256 65,536 ....

WHO IS IT?
Age 10+

Players Group

EQUIPMENT
Paper and pencil for each player, a good pile of photographs of famous people cut out from newspapers and magazines, and some card.

PREPARATION
The host should have cut out part of each photograph so that it shows the eyes only. Each should then be stuck onto the card. Each picture should now be labelled with a number or letter, and a note, kept by the organiser, of the celebrity whose eyes feature in each picture. Each player should also get a list of the celebrities.

PLAYING
- The 'eyes' are passed around the table, and everyone has to write down the name of the personality to whom they belong.
- The winner is the participant making the most correct guesses.

Index